Kentucky Hero
SERIES

Ring The
Silver Bell

The Alice Slone Story

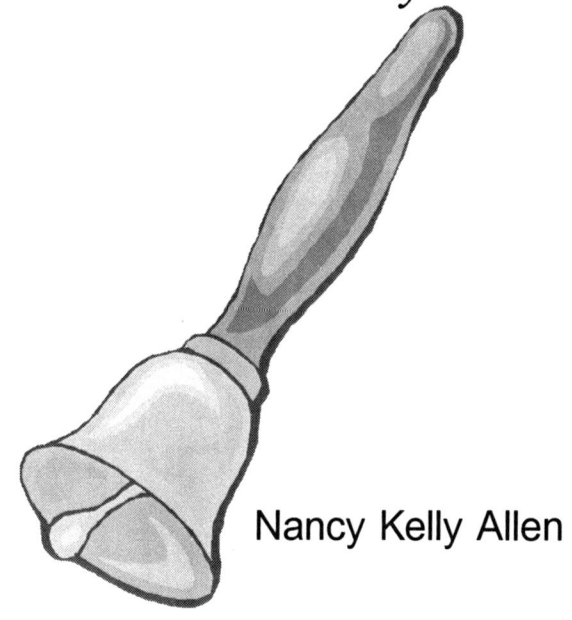

Nancy Kelly Allen

Motes Books
Think Young Collection

RING THE SILVER BELL
The Alice Slone Story

Nancy Kelly Allen

© 2008
ALL RIGHTS RESERVED

ISBN 978-1-934894-06-4
BIOGRAPHY

The publisher and the author wish to thank Alice Whitaker
for generously providing and granting permission to use historic images
from both Alice Slone's personal collection and Cordia School

The publisher acknowledges Jason Howard
for his significant editorial contributions to this book

No portion of this book may be copied, transmitted, duplicated, stored or distributed in any form
(including but not limited to print, mechanical, audio, video, digital or electronic means),
except for brief excerpts used in reviews or commentaries,
without prior express written permission from both the author and the publisher

Front & back cover photos
ANN ANTHONY BACON

Book design
EK LARKEN

Published by

Motes Books

Think Young Collection

Louisville, Kentucky

WWW.MOTESBOOKS.COM

for
KELLI & ALICIA

Barnyard at Alice's family home

Chapter 1
EARLY YEARS

In the horse and buggy days, deep in the Kentucky hills, Alice Slone entered this world on May 4, 1904, just as the moon began its journey across the starlit sky.

Alice's parents, Isaac and Leanner, soon realized that Alice was blessed with a mind keener than a springtime cold snap. As a baby, Alice was curious. She crawled on the cabin floor looking at a spray of spilt salt. As a toddler, she waddled around the porch peeking at Leanner's roses. As a young girl, she chased butterflies through the front yard, hoping to catch a closer look.

When Alice learned to talk, questions poured out of her mouth. "Why are some roses red and others yellow? What makes the wind blow?"

Leanner and Isaac always tried to answer her questions, but sometimes they didn't know the answers themselves. Questions came as natural to Alice as breathing.

Alice loved playing with her older sisters – Lou Hettie, Frankie Jane, and Rilda. More often than not, a smile crossed Alice's face and a twinkle caught in her sky-blue eyes.

As Alice grew taller, her family grew larger. By the

time she was six years old, three more children – Jim Courtney, Bob and Bertha – blessed the family.

Alice's family needed more space so they moved to a small patch of farmland on Caney Creek, just a few miles from where she was born. The valley snuggled deep inside the surrounding mountains.

Isaac built a two-room log cabin with a dogtrot (an outdoor hallway) leading to the kitchen and smokehouse. The puncheon floor – logs split in half, placed close together with the split side up – helped keep the cabin warm in winter. Leanner stored the foodstuff in the small attic above the kitchen. Alice loved to climb the ladder up to the attic. With a bag of seeds in one hand and the other hand gripping the ladder slats, Alice scaled up the wall.

Alice and her family slept in the two-room cabin. Sleeping a distance from the kitchen and smokehouse was safer and more comfortable – in summer the kitchen stayed too hot for sleeping. Wood shutters covered the square openings in the cabin wall. Alice often opened the shutters to let in a cool breeze at night, but the windows had no glass, so mosquitoes and gnats made their home inside the cabin, too.

Living on the farm meant everyone worked, even the children. While Alice hoed the garden, she asked, "Is this plant cabbage or a weed?"

"A weed," Leanner answered. "This is cabbage." Leanner pointed to a broad-leaf plant.

The workday began before the morning sun peeped over the valley and chased the fog from the meadow. Alice spent much of her time with her mother.

As they cooked breakfast, Leanner said, "There is a

lesson to be learned in everything you do."

Lessons came often as Alice learned how to bake biscuits and weave cloth; how too care for sick and injured animals; how to read the newspapers the family pasted on the walls to keep out summer heat and winter cold.

Alice churned buttermilk every day. After Leanner milked the cow, Alice placed the milk in a warm place to clabber. A few hours later, Alice poured the clabbered milk into the churn. She worked the dasher up and down, again and again. As her right arm grew tired, she switched the handle of the dasher to her left hand but kept the dasher moving. When buttermilk formed, Alice scooped the butter off the top of the milk and placed it in a bowl. Leanner help Alice pour the buttermilk from the churn to the special bucket with a lid. Alice tied a rope onto the bucket handle and lowered it down the well to keep the milk cool for supper.

When her older sisters worked with Leanner, Alice had the job of caring for her younger brothers and sister. Her older brother, Commodore, worked with Isaac outdoors. Isaac and Commodore spent each day cutting logs for firewood, digging coal for the fireplace, clearing a newground for the garden, planting crops in the fields, shearing sheep, hunting wild game, and tanning hides.

After dinner on hot summer days, Isaac sat on a ladder-back chair in the dogtrot. He would lean the chair on two legs against the wall to rest for a few minutes. Alice perched on the floor beside him as they talked.

"I saw a hummingbird this morning," Alice said. "Right over there by the rose bush," she pointed toward the red flowers growing near the porch. "The first one I've seen this year."

"A hummingbird, huh?" Isaac said. "Nothing prettier, that's for sure."

"Except maybe for your daughters," Alice joked.

"Right you are, young lady," Isaac said with a chuckle. He didn't sit long, though; he had a field of corn to hoe before supper. No matter how much work Isaac did, he went to bed each night thinking of all the things he didn't get done.

Alice looked forward to the time her family spent together after supper. Her mother sat at the spinning wheel spinning wool and her father busied himself spinning stories as he fixed a horse's harness or wove bark for the seat of a hickory-splint chair. "Did I ever tell you about the time I went bear hunting up by Old Man Jacob's place over on Beaver Creek?"

Alice settled in for an adventure tale that grew bigger each time she heard it. She hung on to every word her father told and imagined traveling along on the journeys. He told of building a raft of logs and floating it down the river to Catlettsburg to sell hides. He told the story of his family's journey with Daniel Boone as they made their way into Kentucky from Virginia. He even entertained the children with stories of knights and kings and a princess or two.

Isaac's tales fascinated Alice, and she wondered if she would ever travel to faraway places. She and her siblings listened to the stories and munched on caps – corn popped in the hot coals of the fireplace.

Stories in books fascinated Alice, too. She learned to read when she was five, and she read books at every opportunity. When she had finished everything readable in her home, she called upon her neighbors who gladly loaned her the few books they had.

Reading carried Alice to faraway places, but when she closed the covers of her book, she enjoyed the company of her family. Alice felt safe in her secure world, but her world would soon be shattered and changed forever.

Alice's brother plows ground for the family garden

Chapter 2
HARD TIMES

One morning in May, Isaac grabbed an axe from the back porch and trekked up the mountain to clear a newground. He worked hour after hour cutting trees to clear the land for a garden. After he cut the trees, Isaac placed a cant-hook on a log to move it. The hook snapped and struck him in the face, crushing his cheekbone.

Isaac walked back home injured and in pain. Leanner immediately cleaned the wound and helped her husband to bed. Isaac needed rest and quiet, but with five children less than eight years of age, quiet wasn't possible in the two-room cabin.

Fear consumed Alice as she waited for her father to heal. She tried being quiet, but quiet wasn't in her nature. Instead, Alice talked, not so much because she wanted to; she had to. She talked to her sisters and brothers. She talked to her mother. If no one was around, she talked to herself. For Alice, talking was the only way she could handle her fear.

Neighbors came to visit and talked in whispers. The whispers nurtured Alice's fears; she asked rapid-fire questions about her father's condition. "Is he worse? Will his cheek heal? Will he live?"

Alice and her family stood by helplessly, watching Isaac suffer unbearable pain. The infection grew worse. He died after a week of tormenting pain.

Losing her father, the gentle man who told stories, who listened to her, who answered her questions, devastated Alice. Alice's grief deepened as she blamed herself for his death. Maybe if she had been a little quieter, he would have lived. Maybe if she hadn't talked so much, he would have gotten better.

After Isaac died, Leanner worked twice as hard to feed the family. Alice and her brothers and sisters worked twice as hard, too, just to help the family survive. Together, Alice's family became tougher than the hard times.

In the few minutes of each day when Alice wasn't pulling weeds from the garden or caring for younger siblings, she headed to the woods. On the hillsides overlooking lush meadows, Alice wandered through the trees to step away from the harsh realities of life. Nature fascinated her.

"I wonder how these wild violets got here," she thought, as she peered at purple flowers clinging to life, against all odds, in the crevice of a cliff. A few minutes later, her heart pitter-pattered with delight at the sight of a hummingbird flying backward. When she walked into a clearing and saw a doe with her spotted fawn standing still as statues, Alice whispered, "Law me," and gazed at the beauty of the deer.

As Alice sat in the shadow of a dogwood tree, her fanciful imagination roamed free. She became anything her heart desired, from a princess to a grand lady. She traveled to kingdoms far away. Her mind overflowed with questions.

She rolled her eyes toward the heavens and asked, "Why is the sky blue?" She looked at water running down a stream and wondered aloud, "How does water get to the top of the mountain?" She pondered questions on every hillside journey.

Alice never spent as much time in the woods as she wanted because Leanner needed her to keep a watchful eye on the younger children. One day she took them to a cliff to play as Leanner and Rilda hoed corn nearby. While her brothers, Jim Courtney and Bob, played and baby Bertha slept, Alice looked around the cliff. She saw a hollow log perched against a large rock. Alice wondered what might be in the log. She got down on her hands and knees to peek. Suddenly, she gasped.

"Mama, here's a copperhead! No, it's a rattlesnake! No, it a garter! No, it's a viper!" Alice squealed, as she kept her eyes locked on the snake.

"Run, Alice!" Leanner yelled.

Alice stood by the log, peeking inside, more curious than scared.

Leanner rushed over and pushed Alice aside. With her hoe handle, Leanner hauled the snake out of the hollow log. Alice gazed at the garter snake as her mother tossed it over the hillside.

By the time Alice was nine years old, she was also responsible for building the fire in the cook stove for supper. Some days, hot coals lingered in the ashes from cooking dinner; other days the ashes were cold.

Alice dreaded building a fire with cold ashes. First, she had to find a mouse's nest. The nests held bits of cotton and shredded pieces of bark. Next, she turned the stove lid on its edge beside the nest. Then, she would hold the flint close to the nest and strike, strike, strike. Finally, with luck, a spark would fly into the nest and start a fire.

One afternoon when Alice stirred the ashes, not one smidgen of an ember glowed in the stove. She looked for a mouse's nest but couldn't locate one. Alice grabbed a bucket and sprinted to the closest neighbor's house, about a mile away. "Might I borrow a chunk of fire?" she asked, breathing hard. The neighbor obliged. With hot coals safely stored in her bucket, she dashed back home to get a blaze going in the cook stove. By the time she returned, Alice was gasping for breath, but there was no time to rest. She was late with the fire and her mother needed to start supper. Alice set the chunk of hot coals in the stove and soon the flames flickered. She looked outside for Leanner but didn't see her. "The stove's ready to cook supper," Alice yelled to her mother.

"I'm here," Leanner answered, as she called from the house they used for sleeping.

Alice walked over to the cabin and saw her mother lying on the bed. She had never seen her hard-working mother stop to rest in the middle of the afternoon, not for any reason.

"What's wrong?" Alice asked in a whisper.

"It's this terrible headache," Leanner answered with her right arm resting on her eyes to block out all light.

Alice trembled. Her mother's words struck like a thumping fist. Was she losing her mother, too? Her heart felt like it just might pound right out of her chest.

Alice's brother plows a hillside garden

Students from long ago pose in front of the school young Alice attended

Chapter 3
THE THREE R'S: READING, 'RITING, & 'RITHMETIC

Much to Alice's relief, Leanner felt well the next morning. Alice dressed and helped her younger sister and brothers get ready for the first day of school.

Carrying her bread-and-milk lunch in a lard pail, Alice skipped along the winding road to the one-room schoolhouse. School was a place where questions were asked and answers found. Alice brimmed with questions. "Where does the white go when snow melts? Why do roots grow down and shoots grow up?" Alice knew where to find the answers – books. School was the place to find books. She itched to hold the books that answered her questions.

The younger children in the primer sat on a bench. Alice and her sister, Rilda, sat at desks with the older students. Her brother, Commodore, was the teacher.

Commodore expected students to be quiet and obedient in his classroom, especially those students who happened to be his brothers and sisters. Before the morning classes ended, Alice decided that Commodore expected more of his brothers and sisters than he did of the other students.

She listened as Commodore explained, "I expect your work to be neater, your answers to be correct, and your behavior to be top-notch." The expression on her brother's face left no room for argument.

Alice knew Commodore would tell Leanner if they misbehaved or didn't complete assignments. Leanner would not be pleased.

Alice sat quietly and memorized. Then she and the other students said their lessons out loud, all at once. Alice liked going to a blab school, where lessons were blabbed. Blabbing was noisy but learning was fun. She remembered reading that Abraham Lincoln attended a blab school, too.

Alice practiced holding her pen just right. She dipped the pen in ink and made fancy letters, taking extra care to prevent drips.

"I refuse to accept messy papers," Commodore said as he handed out complaints when ink drops smeared an otherwise perfectly good paper.

Ink smeared easily, so Alice practiced hour after hour. The pens leaked and ink usually dripped. Drips on paper forced Alice to start over again.

Every day, Alice looked forward to reading class, her favorite. A small, book-lined shelf behind the pot-bellied stove made up the school library. "Well," she would say to Rilda, "I've read all those books, so now I'll enjoy reading them again."

Alice especially loved poetry books. When she didn't have a poem to read, Alice took pen in hand and wrote one of her own.

> *Sing a song of silver sails*
> *Floating in the breeze,*
> *Polly picked a purple pear*
> *To plant among the trees.*

Pupils took turns ringing the silver bell to start school. Every day, Alice crossed her fingers hoping Commodore would call on her. Every day, he selected another student. For the first two weeks of school, Alice kept hoping and crossing her fingers. Every day, her hopes died. Finally, Commodore called her name. Alice held the small bell in her hand and shook it back and forth. The tinny-sounding tinkle sent a tickle down her spine.

Alice forgot about lessons at lunchtime. She and her family usually brought milk and bread or biscuits and ham. One day Alice's younger brother, Jim Courtney, traded his biscuits and ham for a lump of brown sugar and a few crackers. Brown sugar had to be bought at a store, so Alice's family seldom tasted such a treat.

By the time Alice sat down to eat, her brother, Jim Courtney, had eaten his lunch. "I'm still hungry," Jim complained.

Alice opened her lunch pail and began to eat. "You shouldn't trade your biscuit and ham, not even for a lump of brown sugar."

Jim Courtney rolled his big eyes up at Alice. She took a couple of bites, then shared her biscuit and ham with her hungry brother. Alice's lesson with Jim Courtney was lost. He traded his lunch again the very next day – once again, for brown sugar.

"I'm still hungry," Jim complained.

"Oh, Jim Courtney, what am I going to do with you?" Alice asked, as she halved her lunch with her brother.

Each year of school for Alice was better than the last. Schoolwork satisfied her curiosity. She learned about people and places and dreamed of visiting them someday. She learned how to write letters and different kinds of poems. What she didn't enjoy was arithmetic. "These problems are a mystery to me," Alice would mumble. Try as she might, she could not master ciphering.

School lasted three months a year. During the months the children did not attend school, Leanner worked with them on reading, writing, and arithmetic at home. For Alice, reading and writing seemed more like fun than school. When Alice ciphered math problems, she often got the wrong answers. When she drew a map of Europe, she didn't always label the countries and seas with their correct names. However, when Alice wrote she pondered each word, especially when she penned a poem:

> *Thank you for the glorious daffodils.*
> *Beyond their beauty,*
> *Thanks for the gold and white*
> *Of friendly thought.*

She wrote the words and read them aloud to anyone who would listen. Sometimes her brothers and sisters listened; sometimes they had other things to do, or at least pretended to.

"Let me help you with your lesson," Alice would say to her younger siblings. She enjoyed teaching them to read. She even taught them to write poetry, when they would let her.

At night, Alice curled up in a corner and read by the

light of a coal oil lamp, or a tallow candle, and sometimes by the light of the dancing flames in the hearth. Problem was, she had read every book in the house several times. In good weather if there was a horse in the barn, Alice saddled it and rode it to a neighbor's house to borrow a book.

Leanner insisted on good manners and proper behavior from each of her children. So when Alice rode a horse, Leanner expected her to be a lady and ride the horse sidesaddle. Alice didn't like to ride ladylike on a sidesaddle; she like to ride a horse astride, the way her brothers did, or even bareback with no saddle on the horse at all. To stay out of trouble, Alice rode sidesaddle until she got out of sight of her house, then she straddled the horse, one leg on each side. On the return trip, she switched her riding style to sidesaddle just as she rounded the path in sight of her house.

One day, Alice walked into their cabin with her borrowed book and found a cozy spot to curl up. Her eyes scanned the words, but she couldn't concentrate. Instead, she wondered about the changes in her life that were sure to come. Leanner was getting married.

Daddy Wes, Leanner, and the family
(Alice stands at right in white dress with dark belt)

Chapter 4
FUN & GAMES

When Alice was ten years old, Leanner married a neighbor, Wesley Reynolds. Alice liked her stepfather, who was friendly and loved telling stories. She and her brothers and sisters soon began calling him Daddy Wes.

The Slone clan got more than a stepfather when Leanner married. They got stepbrothers and stepsisters too. The family grew larger but the workload grew less. Wesley worked hard around the farm, taking over much of the work in the fields and caring for the animals.

The Slone and Reynolds children had chores to keep them busy, but they didn't have to work from morning until night. Once again, Alice had time to enjoy games and a romp through the woods.

Alice's burning itch for adventure flamed higher. She now had free time and spent it hiking. Hikes could be dangerous since bears and wildcats made their homes in those hills. Leanner taught Alice how to whittle a stick and use it to keep a fierce animal at bay.

Alice enjoyed walks through patches of black-eyed Susans and wild irises. "Just smell the sweet honeysuckle vines," she would say to her brothers and sisters when they went along. Alice delighted in the colorful paintbrush of nature. Sometimes she spread her arms and pretended she was an eagle as her imagination soared away on a new adventure.

Leanner had some worries of her own about Alice's ventures into the woods, especially when Alice slipped off alone without telling anyone where she was going. As she traipsed through the woods, Alice had no fear. She climbed rocks to see what might be in the crevice near the top. She clung with fingers and toes to the steep cliff as she crawled around the rocky ridges. Sore knuckles and bruised knees didn't stop her from battling the crooks and crannies of a rugged hillside.

By the time Alice found her way home, Leanner was often wringing her hands with worry. On those occasions, Leanner gave Alice a switching and, for good measure, a talking-to that lasted much longer than Alice wanted to hear.

The next day Alice headed right back to the hills. Roots fascinated her. She wondered what the roots of plants looked like. She dug roots and held them in her hand as she studied their shapes and textures and colors. "What is the adventure in digging a root if I can't taste it?" she wondered. If the taste of the root held promise, she dug more and brought them home with her. Maybe her mother would know what they were and how to fix them for supper.

Alice gathered berries and nuts, too. Butternuts and chestnuts topped the list of favorites. She picked persimmons after the frost had wrinkled their skins and made them sweet. Mulberries and gooseberries grew all around the mountain. On the top of the ridge, bushes dripped with ever-so-sweet huckleberries. And in the late summer, Alice prowled through the hills searching for paw-paw trees. For her, nothing matched the taste of a sweet, ripe paw-paw. Just the thought of that banana-flavored custard set Alice's mouth to watering. She usually ate her fill and then picked all she could carry for her brothers and sisters.

Since Commodore was grown, Rilda, Bob, Jim, Bertha, and the Reynolds siblings often roamed the hills and valleys with Alice. When they banded together for fun and games, mischief wasn't far behind.

One of their favorite games required a code of sibling honor. "You mustn't tell Mama and Daddy Wes," Alice would say as she searched for a forked stick. The kids would then creep with hushed steps through the trees and underbrush until they found a snake. Alice, with the speed of a blink, thrust the forked end of the stick behind the head of the snake so it couldn't strike and bite them. She reached her hand behind the head of the snake and picked it up. After stroking the snake a few times, she released it back to the wild. "Isn't that curious?" she said each time, and the game started over again with another of the Slone or Reynolds clan capturing a different snake.

When they sneaked away from Leanner in the fall of the year, smoking corncob pipes topped their list of favorite things to do. The process began with a short piece of a corncob. Using a hot poker, they bored holes in one side and one end of the cob. Alice stuck a hollow stem into the side hole and filled the top hole with dried corn silks.

"Now light it, Rilda," she would say. They coughed

more than they smoked, but coughing simply added to the fun.

Yellow clay dug from a nearby clay hole was used to chink their log house. Chinking filled the gaps between the logs. One day when Alice and her siblings finished their chores early, Alice said, "Let's pinch off pieces of clay and write on the logs." Later that afternoon when Leanner saw their handiwork, she threatened them with a switching. They promised never to write on the logs again. So instead of writing on logs, the Slone clan grabbed chinks of clay when Leanner was out of sight and headed to the hills to write on rocks. If they were careful in the manner in which they pinched off the clay, a hole would not be visible. Usually, Leanner didn't find the area of missing clay until the dead of winter. By then, every child denied all charges.

When cold or rainy weather settled around the little cabin, the children holed up like groundhogs waiting for the sun to come out. Winter was a time when there was little work for them to do. The winter days were short and the nights were long. They sat around the fireplace and told stories and sang songs. Alice's favorite was the English ballad, Barb'ry Allen.

On Saturday evenings, Alice's family visited kinfolk that lived nearby. The kids played outside or sat around a fire inside and listened to more stories, sometimes until darkness gripped hold. On those nights, they grabbed a couple of pine knots kept in a basket near the front door and lit the resin in the pine knots that burned slowly, throwing off just enough torchlight for them to see the path as they walked home.

Alice enjoyed the short adventures over a hill to the neighbor's house. Soon, however, a long adventure would lead her out of the hills to a land flat as the back of her hand.

Chickens perch on the barnyard fence

Alice in Cleveland

Ann Anthony Bacon

Chapter 5
ALICE'S DREAM

By the time Alice finished eighth grade, she hadn't learned everything she wanted to learn. She hadn't read everything she wanted to read. She had studied all the arithmetic she wanted to study, but in her heart, she knew she needed to learn to cipher better.

A deep yearning tugged at Alice, nudging her to attend high school. The real world held no high school close by, and her family had no money for boarding school. After finishing eight grades, most of the children Alice's age went to work helping their parents on the farm. Alice had heard about high schools, but had never seen one. No high schools existed within walking distance of her home. No roads existed either, just foot paths and horse trails.

Alice had also heard of automobiles, but none ever made it to her valley. "We're not likely to see one, either," Alice told Bertha. "The only roads around here are creek beds and foot paths." Alice figured she was as likely to ride in an automobile as she was to continue her education. With each passing day, Alice's hopes of going to high school dimmed like the last flicker of candlelight.

Alice had no interested in staying on the farm. "I want adventure," she said. "I want to meet new people." She was curious and filled with questions that her education still hadn't answered. "Do people far from here have the same dreams I have? How is city life different from that of the farm? What do I want to do with the rest of my life?"

Alice had an ambition different from that of Leanner, whose goal in life was to establish a home and raise her children. Her mother understood that difference and even encouraged it.

Leanner wanted her daughter to go to high school, but as much as Leanner desired an education for Alice, she had no means of providing it. Alice's disappointment weighed heavily on Leanner's mind. She knew education held the key to a better life for Alice, as well as for all her children. "I don't want your dreams to die, Alice," Leanner said. "I've heard about a woman who might help."

So, one day, Leanner and Alice rode horses to the Caney Creek Community Center. There they saw a grand lady step down from a carriage unlike any Alice had ever seen.

Alice was awestruck. "She must be a princess!" Alice said to Leanner. All her life she had heard such stories, but she never really expected to meet a real, live princess with a fancy carriage. Alice's pulse raced as she watched the lady.

"The woman is Mrs. Lloyd, who came from Massachusetts and opened this community center," Leanner explained with a smile.

Alice and her mother met with Mrs. Lloyd, who talked with Alice and soon realized that Alice was serious about getting a high school and college education. Alice's vision was clear. "I am going to work to pay my way," Alice declared. After all, she was no stranger to work. "I'm ready to do whatever it takes to make my dream come true."

Mrs. Lloyd believed that leadership in the mountains needed to come from people living in the mountains, and she saw that Alice had the drive and commitment to be a leader. "Alice, your potential needs to be developed," Mrs. Lloyd said, "and education is the key."

By the time the meeting was over, Alice's dream trickled on. Mrs. Lloyd gave her some clothes and a chance to go to high school in Cleveland, Ohio. "You can stay with a family and go to school during the day," Mrs. Lloyd explained. In the evenings and on weekends Alice would work for the family to pay for her room and board. Mrs. Lloyd had made it possible for Alice to live her dream. The woman, who Alice first thought was a princess, now seemed more like a fairy godmother.

Purpose Road was the name Mrs. Lloyd used to explain her mission. She had a purpose in getting Alice educated, and that purpose was for Alice to come back to the mountains and work if Mrs. Lloyd ever asked her to. Alice agreed.

"Naturally, I want to return home to my family when I graduate," Alice said. "Oh, I want to visit other places, but Caney Creek is home."

Leanner said she was worried about Alice traveling to a distant place and living with strangers. "But at the same time," Leanner told her daughter, "I know leaving home is the only chance you'll have to get an education." Leanner wanted all her children to have an easier life than she had endured.

At the tender age of thirteen, Alice understood that

she could achieve her dream if she worked hard. She also understood that without her mother's intervention, her life would have taken a very different course.

When Alice left for Ohio, Commodore handed her fifteen dollars! "I've never had so much money in my life," she marveled. "Glory be! From Commodore, at that."

Alice thought of how long Commodore must have worked to earn that money. How much he sacrificed to give her such a gift. Now she realized why he accepted nothing but the best from them: Commodore wanted his brothers and sisters to be the best they could become. With tears in her eyes and a lump in her throat, Alice waved good-bye to her family.

A bumpy twelve-mile ride on a jolt wagon took an excited thirteen-year-old Alice to Wayland to catch a train. "The ride is rough," Alice thought, "but the future looks smooth."

The locomotive slowly puffed through the narrow valleys and snaked along the mountains to where the land leveled out. The flat countryside looked as if the mountains had rolled over and lain down.

Doubts, as black as the smoke from the locomotive that chugged up the tracks, began to cloud Alice's excitement. "Who are these people I will live with?" she questioned herself. "What if they don't like me? What if they are impossible to live with?"

Doubts about being different: "Will I look different? Act different? Talk different?"

Doubts about living in a city: "Is it dangerous? Will I get lost?"

Doubts about living away from her family plagued her.

That was the hardest part – she wondered when she would see them again.

Even with the doubts, Alice tingled with delight.

Alice when she first arrived in Cleveland

Alice at Susan B. Anthony's house in New York

Ann Anthony Bacon

Chapter 6
A NEW LIFE

Alice settled in her new home with the family of Ann Anthony Bacon. Immediately, she liked Mrs. Bacon, who was the niece of Susan B. Anthony, the suffragist who worked to get women the right to vote. Alice especially liked Mrs. Bacon's attitude that girls should get an education and use that education to make a living. Alice noticed that Mrs. Bacon stayed true to her beliefs; she made her living as a photographer.

However, Alice wasn't as impressed with Mrs. Bacon's three daughters, who were near her own age. She had hoped that girls in the home would make her stay more enjoyable; however, she soon realized that was not to be. She wanted to talk with the girls and spend time with them. She missed her brothers and sisters and thought the Bacon girls could help ease the longing. The sisters refused to associate with her. Alice asked herself why. "Is it because I am poor? Do they consider me just a servant?" Alice wanted to be a friend to them and couldn't understand why they didn't feel the same way.

Alice was thankful that Mrs. Bacon was polite to her as she explained the chores she expected Alice to do, but Mrs. Bacon had little else to say. Alice stayed busy cleaning the house, washing and ironing, and working in the kitchen. She decided that staying busy was the best cure for homesickness.

Alice focused on the positive. She enjoyed the new refinements in her life: fine food, an elegant house, and a constant display of manners, even in the way people spoke and walked. She quickly learned that Mrs. Bacon had certain social standards that she insisted everyone meet, especially in her house. Since Alice was a servant, she entered and left the Bacon household through the back door.

At school, Alice was just as busy. She took a placement test and had no problems with writing. She raced through the reading section with ease. What didn't seem easy was the next part – arithmetic. Alice struggled with the numbers. She multiplied. She divided. She counted. She tried, but she just couldn't figure out the right answers.

As she expected, Alice did well in the writing and reading portions of the test. In fact, she scored much higher than other eighth grade students. As Alice also expected, despite her best efforts, scores on the arithmetic section left much to be desired.

Alice was deeply disappointed when her teachers suggested that she repeat the eighth grade. She had dreamed of going to high school for so long. Now, just when it seemed her dream was coming true, she had lost it. She felt like Cinderella at midnight; she had been a princess for a little while, but reality set in.

A little setback now and then was just part of life, Alice soon decided. She enrolled at Prospect Grade School and worked every night on lessons. Arithmetic didn't come easily for her, but she learned, lesson by lesson. She soon realized that repeating the eighth grade was to her advantage. Her grades were good and slowly but surely her understanding of arithmetic improved.

Alice missed her family and wrote to them often. She told them about her new home and the family she lived with. "Cleveland is different from Caney Creek," she explained. "Flat land. Houses close together. Roads. Crowds of people." Most of all, she delighted in telling Leanner how pleased her teachers were with her progress.

Nothing excited Alice more than getting a letter from home. Three weeks after she left Kentucky, she received not only a letter but a package, too. She opened the letter from Leanner and read it. Alice was delighted that everyone at home was well, and her heart tugged when she read that everyone missed her. "I miss them just as much," Alice whispered as she tore into the box filled to the rim with delicious chestnuts.

At the Bacon house, Alice stayed busy. When she wasn't cleaning and working for Mrs. Bacon, she studied, read books and wrote poetry. Alice thought about the family she missed and the mountains she called home. She thought about how much her mother loved her – enough to set her free to discover the world – and she wrote:

> *Love*
> *Brush lightly!*
> *With butterfly wings,*
> *Bless and release,*
> *Never binding,*
> *Never constraining,*
> *Love is a freedom thing.*

Alice appreciated the opportunity her mother gave her to get a high school education. "I don't care how hard I have to work or how long it takes," she said. "I will do it." She knew she could. She dreamed of nothing else.

Month after month, Alice tried to build friendships with the Bacon sisters, but they hardly noticed her. Alice's accent made her different. Her few clothes were plain and simple, in contrast to the fancy, tailored type worn by the Bacons.

The following spring, Alice listened as the Bacon sisters decided to go to the Northway Lodge, a wilderness girl's camp in Ontario, Canada. The girls talked about the fun they would have that summer, the people they would meet, and the beauty of the wilderness. The cost of going to the exclusive camp was expensive, but the family could afford it.

Alice's spirit for adventure was as keen as ever. She wanted to go to that camp too, but she had no money. She decided there must be a way to go if only she could think of it.

Alice dreamed of the camp as she washed dishes. She thought of ways to make money as she mopped the floors. She considered different plans as she washed the clothes and made the beds. As she ironed dresses, an inkling of idea took form. That very evening Alice wrote a letter to the camp's director offering to work to pay her way. Her willingness to work had made dreams come true before; maybe it would again.

Alice watched the mailbox. A few days later, a letter from the camp arrived. She held it in her hand and wondered if the news would be good. Would she be accepted at

Northway Lodge? She was almost afraid to read the letter, afraid the news would not be what she wanted. At last, Alice opened the envelope. She trembled as she read the words, not believing her good luck. The camp director agreed to pay her way to the camp! She would be working, but she was off on a new adventure.

"What in the world will happen next?" she wondered.

Alice at Northway Lodge wilderness camp in Canada

Alice at wilderness camp in Canada

Ann Anthony Bacon

Chapter 7
A SUMMER CAMP

The first day at the wilderness camp, Alice went to work. When Mrs. Fannie L. Case, the camp director, said, "Your job will be in the kitchen," Alice knew she could handle it.

"I've always helped my mother cook the meals," Alice explained, "and for the last year, I've spent much of my time in Mrs. Bacon's kitchen."

To her surprise, though, Alice's job was not cooking. She scrubbed pots and pans. Not one to let disappointment get her down, she focused on her wonderful opportunity of going to camp. What Alice hadn't counted on was how large the kettles were. How heavy. How many.

Scrubbing pots and pans was hot and tiring. Beads of sweat ran down Alice's face as she reached for another pot to clean, but she wiped the sweat off her brow with the back of her hand and kept on scrubbing. The stack of pots sometimes seemed as tall as the mountains back home on Caney Creek. Pot by pot, that mountain flattened as Alice scrubbed, long into the afternoon.

Alice didn't complain about the work. Instead, she concentrated on what she would do afterward. "A brisk walk in the woods to breathe the air of the cool breeze always lifts my spirits," she told a fellow camper. "I think I'll sit on a rock overlooking a waterfall and ponder my future." Excursions through the woods were always exciting. And there were archery lessons. She loved the feel of the bow in her hand as she released an arrow. Zing! Alice practiced so much that she could hit the bull's-eye more often than not.

Mrs. Case often came by the kitchen to check on Alice. Sometimes in the evenings when the work was done, Alice and the director talked about life. At first, the conversations were short, but as they became more acquainted, the visits grew longer.

"Alice, you have that *special something*," the director told her. "Something in the way you work until the job is finished; something in the pride you take in a job well done; something in the way you work with people; something in the way you never complain."

Alice appreciated the respect and compliments Mrs. Case passed her way. Alice was especially pleased that the director promised her the job as a counselor in next summer's camp.

The Canadian wilderness reminded Alice of the Kentucky hills. In her free time she rambled through the beautiful woods, identifying plants. If she happened upon a snake, she used a forked stick to secure the snake's head as she picked up the creature. She stroked it a few times and set it free. As usual, she carefully chose nonpoisonous snakes to pick up, steering away from copperheads and rattlesnakes.

Sitting on a log near a sparkling stream, Alice pulled a small notebook and pen out of her pocket. She looked up at the tall trees surrounding her and set her thoughts to paper.

The lone pine is a tall thin sigh
Trailing its urgency to the sky.

Alice was disappointed that the time spent at the camp with the Bacon sisters didn't improve her relationship with them. When Alice attempted to talk with the girls, they spoke but had no more to say. Alice wondered, "Do I embarrass them? After all, I do have to wash dishes to pay my way. Maybe they don't want to be seen with someone who has to work to go to camp." But Alice refused to allow herself to be troubled by something that was beyond her control. Instead, Alice talked and worked with other girls at the camp and became friends with many of them.

"I do hope when we return to Ohio, those Bacon sisters will be a little friendlier," she thought. Alice longed for their friendship and acceptance and vowed to keep trying to win them over.

Alice in Cleveland at Rockefeller Park

Ann Anthony Bacon

Chapter 8
LIVING A DREAM

At the end of summer, Alice and the Bacon girls returned to Cleveland. As hard as she tried, Alice still had not developed a friendship with them.

As soon as Alice returned to the Bacon household, work awaited her. Once again, she cleaned floors, cooked, washed, and ironed clothes all day long. For Alice, each chore was worth the effort, because the time had come for her to enter high school.

The first day she walked through the high school doors, Alice had to force herself to take deep breaths. Excitement washed over her like a tide in a mountain stream. "I feel like I'm living a fairy tale," she thought, "and once again I am the princess." Shaw High School was huge, nothing like the small one-room school back on Caney Creek. And fancy – made of bricks. She realized the exclusive high school was designed for children of wealth.

Alice stood just inside the door and drank in the scene: tall ceilings, long hallways, large rooms, students walking in small groups, laughter. She loved it all and silently thanked her mother and Mrs. Lloyd for making it all possible.

"I know I am different," Alice thought. She looked

different in her plain clothes. She sounded different, with her mountain accent. She could not afford to participate in extracurricular activities. "But no need to dwell on the negative," she decided, and she walked down the hall with her head held high. Her spirit soared.

Within the next few days, Alice settled into the routine of school days. The classes kept her busy, but she enjoyed every minute. Most of all, she relished going to the library. She wandered through the shelves, reading titles on the spines of books. Alice checked out books, read them, returned them, and checked out more. At school, she made friends with many of the students and the days passed rapidly, like flipping a calendar.

High school classes offered Alice a way to understand the questions that flooded her mind. Alice wanted to make good grades, but even more, she wanted to learn as much as she possibly could. Her eagerness to work and learn pleased her teachers. She spent hours in the library reading, researching, and studying. The library was filled with books, and books held the answers to questions she hadn't even thought of yet.

"Sometimes I still can't believe a poor girl from Caney Creek can live in a city and attend high school," Alice often said, reflecting on the changes made in her life in the past year. She felt as though she had entered another world, beginning the day she stepped off the train in Cleveland. She missed the old world but loved the new one. The new world held promises – high school, college, career – that the old world had not.

Alice did not allow herself to feel out of place because she didn't have fancy clothes. She didn't allow herself to feel second best because the Bacon sisters didn't associate with her at school or at home.

Alice appreciated the courteous manner in which Mrs. Bacon treated her. When she wasn't working on chores, Alice spent time in her room completing homework, reading or writing. She was always happy when Mrs. Bacon came in to talk with her about life, about the future, about any problem Alice was having. Sometimes, Mrs. Bacon even shared her own problems with Alice. They shared laughter and tears, time and again. Alice cherished their friendship.

One day when Alice was folding laundry, Mrs. Bacon knocked on her door. Mrs. Bacon's arms were piled high with clothes.

"My daughters have outgrown these," Mrs. Bacon explained kindly. "I'd like to pass them on to you."

Alice appreciated Mrs. Bacon's generosity. "Thank you," slipped out of Alice's mouth over and over as she held up each blouse, each skirt, each scarf and admired it. Alice loved her new finery. She mixed and matched the clothes, adding belts and scarves to skirts and dresses. Alice mixed and matched the items so much, sometimes the Bacon girls didn't recognize the clothes they had once called their own.

"Where did you get those beautiful outfits?" girl after girl at school asked Alice.

When Alice explained that the clothes were hand-me-downs that she had updated, they asked Alice to help them update their clothes, too. Alice's heart thumped with joy as she worked with the girls, showing them how to make an outfit look different by mixing parts of two or three outfits together or adding a jacket. Even more, Alice's heart thumped with joy because she finally felt accepted by the students.

One day Mrs. Bacon asked, "Alice, may I photograph you?"

Alice was overjoyed at having her picture taken by a professional photographer. Alice dressed in Mrs. Bacon's fancy clothes and pranced and posed all afternoon as Mrs. Bacon snapped away with the camera.

Alice adapted to her new life. Mrs. Bacon placed social correctness as top priority, and Alice closely followed her example. Mrs. Bacon's intellectual and artistic life strongly influenced her, as well.

"Sure, I have to work to earn my keep," she thought. "No, I don't have the fancy clothes other students wear, but one thing is certain: I have never been happier!"

As her relationship with Mrs. Bacon warmed, her relationship with the Bacon sisters kindled, as well. Alice invited the sisters to her room, and they came to talk and study and visit. Alice sometimes went with the sisters to social events, and they gradually accepted her into their group at school.

Alice continued to live with the Bacon family, and each year her bond with the sisters grew closer. They spent time together at school, home, and social events. Alice continued to do her chores, but she no longer had to enter and leave the house by the back door.

At her high school graduation, Alice was pleased to see the Bacon family in attendance. "The time has come to move on," Alice told them, "but I will always appreciate the years with my new family in Cleveland."

Alice spent the summer after graduation the same way she had spent each of the last four summers: working at Northway Lodge, the wilderness camp in Canada. She enjoyed her job as a counselor, and her friendship with the camp's director, Mrs. Case, continued to grow.

The summer camp and the friendships Alice made there would eventually help her make a stream of dreams come true.

Alice as an archer

Alice as a young woman

Ann Anthony Bacon

Chapter 9
CONTINUING THE DREAM

After summer camp, Alice enrolled in Boyd Business School. She worked to pay for her education, and enjoyed the challenge of the classes. Academic achievement was important to her, so she studied hard and made good grades. The day she graduated, Alice jumped with joy, but deep inside she still dreamed of attending college. Alice had no money, so a college education seemed impossible. Not one for giving up easily, Alice reminded herself, "Never say *never*."

Once again, she headed out to the wilderness camp in Canada. She spent the summer counseling campers and thinking about what she wanted to do with the rest of her life. As she wandered the woods, enjoying the solitude and beauty, Alice considered her options. She discussed her plans with Mrs. Case, the camp director, who encouraged Alice to go to college.

Alice applied to Ohio State University in Columbus and was accepted. Now all she had to do was find a way to pay for college. She accepted one job working in an office and another job washing dishes to earn money to pay for living expenses and a few classes each semester.

Alice knew she could work her way through college. So what if it took a few more years? "The time and effort will be worth it," Alice thought, remembering the years she spent with the two most influential women in her life. "My mother taught me the value of hard work," she would later say, "and Mrs. Bacon's high social standards provided me a model of etiquette."

Because her workload was so heavy, Alice took only a few classes at a time. Sometimes she had no money to pay for classes. During those times, she worked three different jobs, to save money for school. In the private moments of her life, Alice enjoyed reading and discovering the new worlds she found in books.

One day, Alice heard about a farm in Pennsylvania that needed workers. Nature fascinated her, especially farm animals, so the job seemed perfect. Alice boarded the train and once again headed out on a new adventure.

The work on the farm was just what she expected. She carried water and feed to the animals, tended the crops, and loved the time spent outdoors. Alice discovered something about herself while working on the farm, something she had suspected for a long time: "I would like to spend a lifetime working with animals and plants. Nature is my calling." Alice decided to take courses in agriculture, or maybe animal husbandry, or even forestry when she returned to college.

After Alice worked and saved enough money to return to Ohio State University, she was told that she could not major in animal husbandry, agriculture, or forestry. Those courses were reserved for the male students. "That notion is preposterous," she said. "If I have the money and want to take the classes, I can't understand why I shouldn't be allowed to do so."

By now, Alice had grown tall and lean. She crossed

and uncrossed her long legs as she calmly and logically presented her case. She figured the professors had probably never dealt with so determined a female student in their insulated world. But as she pled her case, the professors stood firm on their decision. Much to her dismay, Alice once again accepted the fact that life was not always fair.

"Well," she decided, "I don't have the luxury of time to dwell upon disappointment." Instead, she promptly began a program of studies in education.

In typical Alice fashion, when she wasn't attending classes, she studied diligently. When she wasn't studying, she worked two jobs to pay for her education.

At Ohio State, Alice met a young man, Paul Zeranger. Paul was handsome and courteous. Soon, she and Paul were spending as much free time together as Alice could find. Their time together was special to Alice, so special that when Paul asked Alice to marry him, she said, "Yes." Alice had known happiness, but none that could equal the time she spent with him.

She enjoyed taking classes with Paul. They always entered the classroom together so they could sit side by side. On day, when the professor became especially long-winded, Paul wrote her a poem and passed it to her.

> *My love is young, my love is fair*
> *My love has dark brown curly hair.*
> *She's sweet and gentle – and oh my dear!*
> *She says the most delightful things.*

Alice read the poem. She noticed that the last two lines didn't rhyme, but she didn't mind. "How sweet," she whispered, looking at Paul with a twinkle in her eye.

Eight years after she entered college, the day for which

Alice had worked so hard finally arrived: graduation day. Once again, she felt like the princess her father had described in the stories he told after supper. She had her plans laid out in her mind, neat and tidy. "I will get a job, marry, and settle down in Ohio to raise a family," she decided.

Alice knew her father would be proud of his little princess if he could see her now. What Alice didn't know was the clock would soon strike midnight. Her enchanted world was about to collapse.

Chapter 10
BACK TO THE MOUNTAINS

A few days after graduation, Alice received a letter from Mrs. Lloyd. Alice read the letter and reread it in disbelief. Mrs. Lloyd, the woman at the community center on Caney Creek who sent Alice to Ohio, was calling her back home.

Alice wondered how she could be expected to leave the man she planned to marry. "Paul will not go to Kentucky to live," she told a friend.

Alice had worked so hard for fifteen years to put herself through school. "Fifteen years! I did it all myself," she cried. "I earned the money. I took the courses. Why shouldn't I do what I want with my life?" She believed that she had earned the right to live where she wanted, to work where she wanted. She had worked hard for the right to make her own choices. "Is it fair to expect me to go back to Caney Creek?" Questions ran through Alice's mind like a runaway train. The answers were nowhere in sight.

Tears welled in Alice's eyes and streamed down her cheeks as she reread the letter once again. At night, she tossed and turned and considered her future: "Can I turn my back on the new life I've come to love? Should I? Whose life am I living anyhow? Should I allow Mrs.

Lloyd to dictate my goals?"

Alice mulled over Mrs. Lloyd's request as she considered the hardships she had faced as an adult and the fresh possibilities of the future. First was the lack of money. She had worked so hard to earn every penny to pay her way through school. Then there was the matter of classes. She would have preferred a degree in which she worked with animals or plants. And she would be leaving the new life she had grown to love, but she would be returning to the life she had loved all along. Finally, the most confusing problem of them all: leaving Paul, the man she planned to marry. She wanted to see her family again, but she didn't want to leave Paul.

Alice discussed the letter from Mrs. Lloyd with Paul and the promise she had made to return to Caney Creek when she completed her education.

"I understand the responsibility to your people," Paul said. He felt the same responsibility to his own family who owned a farm near Columbus. His family expected him to return home to manage the farm, and Paul didn't want to disappoint them.

The more Alice thought about home, the more she considered returning to Caney Creek. She had promised Mrs. Lloyd she would return to the mountains of Kentucky to work, if asked. "And now I have been asked," she said, realizing just how much she would love to see her family. Her brothers and sisters were all grown, even the baby, Bertha. She was happy that her younger brother, Bob, was now working for the Bacon family and going to school.

Day after day, Alice dealt with conflicting feelings. Finally, through tears and doubts, Alice made up her mind to go back to Caney Creek. "After all," she explained to Paul, "a person is no better than her word, and I did promise to return. I just hadn't counted on falling in love with you. Going back to Kentucky doesn't mean I have to stay forever. A year or two and my obligation to Mrs. Lloyd will be fulfilled; then I can return to Ohio."

Alice said good-bye to Paul Zeranger. "I have never taken the easy road in life," she told him, "but of all my choices, this one is the hardest to make and the hardest to live with."

She looked at Paul who hugged her close. "Some things are stronger unsaid – just felt," he whispered. Tears filled his eyes.

Alice's worst fears had now been realized. With sadness, she headed toward Kentucky. "Those mountains must have magnets in them," she thought, as they drew her back home.

That train ride back to Caney Creek in 1932 was filled with more doubts than the ride that had carried her out fifteen years earlier. This time she envisioned what the future held in store: living and working on Caney Creek. She could see no adventure in that.

Still, Alice faced up to her responsibility with a positive outlook. She had survived difficult times and became stronger as she dealt with each new problem. "I'm determined to make life the best it can be," she declared.

As the train snaked in and out of valleys, excitement tracked through Alice as she thought about seeing her mother again. As the train pulled into the station, Alice peeked out the window looking for anyone she knew. As she stepped off the train, Leanner and her youngest brother, Bob, walked up.

Tears streaked down Alice's face as she looked into her mother's eyes for the first time in fifteen years. Her mother had aged, and that was natural, but she appeared to be in good health. So did Bob. Through hugs and tears and tears and hugs, the three Slones smiled and laughed.

"It's been so long since I've seen you," Alice whispered as she hugged her mother.

"Too long," Leanner agreed, hugging her daughter and wiping away tears of her own.

When Alice arrived at Caney Creek, Mrs. Lloyd was pleased with the person Alice had become. "Alice, you left the mountains as a boisterous girl," she said. "You have returned a sophisticated woman."

"A willful woman," Alice thought, but what she said was, "Thank you, Mrs. Lloyd."

Alice was surprised with the development on Caney Creek. The letters from her family had kept her in touch, but she couldn't believe all the changes she saw. Fifteen years ago, the community had a small one-room school. Now, a big six-room grade school, a high school, and even a two-year college opened doors for students. "Mrs. Lloyd," Alice said, "you have been a busy woman."

Alice enjoyed living at home with her mother once again. She and Leanner spend hours together talking about family and life and what the future might hold.

Alice began teaching for Mrs. Lloyd. She was also surprised to discover that she enjoyed her new job. She was glad to be home – and, as she had always done, Alice turned to poetry. She painted a picture of her feelings with words.

But child of impulse
Born of wind-song
Need not explain
To the wild high wind
Why I left the land wren
To seek again.

Alice and Mrs. Lloyd developed mutual respect for each other. Both expected a lot of themselves and had keen intellects. Both knew that education was the key that could unlock the door of poverty for the people. Both commanded enormous self-control and dignity. And, most importantly, both possessed strong ambitions.

Alice agreed with Mrs. Lloyd's philosophy that the students at the Caney Schools could be leaders: "Great works can be done by the people of the mountains." Those words rang true with Alice, who, herself, had become a leader and an inspiration to other students.

Even though Alice liked her new job and enjoyed getting to know her family again, something was missing. "Why, I miss my friends in Ohio and the summer camp in Canada," she said. She wanted more from life than this job offered, but she really wasn't sure what that might be.

Alice's chance for leadership – and a way to find that 'something' in life – came from her baby sister, Bertha. Bertha was teaching at Cordia Grade School. Cordia was a small community in Knott County, about twenty-five miles from Caney Creek. The community didn't have a high school, and Bertha saw the need for one.

Alice listened as Bertha encouraged her to build a high school for the students at Cordia. Alice knew the challenge would be great since she had no money to build a school.

She also remembered how desperately she had wanted an education.

Alice temporarily taught classes in this Masonic Lodge in Knott County, Kentucky

Chapter 11
ALICE'S GREATEST CHALLENGE

For months, Alice considered the idea of building a high school. She read about a program called Hull House in which the community was involved with the education of the students. The idea fascinated Alice, so she took a train to Chicago to visit Hull House and the woman who developed the program, Jane Addams. Alice was so impressed with the work of Jane Addams, she vowed to do the same if she ever built a school.

With Mrs. Lloyd's blessing, the very next year, in 1933, Alice decided to build a high school at Cordia. "I have no inkling of how to carry out such an incredible project," she said.

"One step at a time," Mrs. Lloyd answered.

Alice began her new adventure one step at a time trekking over Hardburly Mountain. As she climbed step by steep step up one side of the hill and eased down the other, Alice observed the lay of the land. As she ended her journey, she noticed Cordia Grade School was situated on Lotts Creek, a small community with hollows that fit together like a jigsaw puzzle. "Roads? There were none," she would later say, "unless the creek bed could be considered a road." A few houses were scattered along the valleys, mostly up hollows. So, with fifty dollars in her pocket and a suitcase in her hand, Alice faced her greatest challenge yet.

At Cordia, she found that money was as scarce as school supplies. She found no building for a school, not even a classroom. She did find seven pupils, ready and waiting.

Alice needed money to build a school, to buy supplies, to teach students. The summers Alice spent at the wilderness camp in Canada began to pay off in full measure. Not only did she develop leadership skills while working at the camp, she also learned how to organize, plan and accomplish a goal, against all odds. Alice looked around Cordia and decided she didn't have to have a school building to teach school.

Cold, wet days took Alice, now called Miss Slone, and her class to the home of Everett Combs who lived nearby. She rang a silver bell to take up books. The first time she rang that bell, a familiar tingle – the same feeling she'd had as a little girl ringing the school bell on Caney Creek – rushed through her. She held classes in a small bedroom. "On warm, sunny days," she announced, "we'll hold class outdoors."

Alice knew she couldn't keep teaching in the small bedroom. "I must find another place," she said. "A larger place." She noticed that a Masonic Lodge built near the elementary school at Cordia was not used on a daily basis. Alice contacted some members of the lodge and got permission to hold classes there until she could get a building constructed.

Alice needed the help of the community to build a school. She focused her energies and called on local people to help. They came willingly. Her action encouraged others in the community to follow suit. Fathers and sons worked side by side clearing the land to build a cabin. Many of the boys were students at Cordia. They wanted a high school for themselves and were ready to build one.

Alice continued to reach out to the community for help. When the land was cleared, Tom Dobson offered to donate trees for the cabin. John Riley Kelly offered to saw the trees into logs at his sawmill. Alice gladly accepted.

When Alice wasn't teaching or working with laborers, she wrote letters. She needed to establish a financial base for the school. She wrote letters to the friends she had made at the wilderness camp in Canada and at the schools she attended in Ohio. She told them about her plans for a settlement school.

"The school will not close its doors when classes are over at the end of the day," she wrote. "The students will live in dormitories through the week if their homes are too far away for them to walk to class. They will receive meals, clothes and other supplies, if they need them."

Alice watched people clear the land, day by day. They cut and sawed logs. She needed building materials, mainly windows, for the cabin. Alice had no extra money and neither did the people of the community. The country was in the midst of the Great Depression. "Hard times are knocking on the doors of mountain families, just as surely as anywhere else," Alice said.

Alice had a plan. She went to Hindman to talk with a banker. Many banks in the United States lost their money and closed their doors permanently when the Depression hit. Banks that stayed in business didn't lend money easily. They needed collateral, such as a house or land, to guarantee they would get their money back.

The banker at Hindman wanted to help Alice. "Do you own a house?" he asked.

Alice explained she didn't own a house; she boarded with a family near Cordia.

"Land?" the banker asked.

Alice explained that she didn't own land. The only collateral she had to offer was her word that she would repay every cent she borrowed.

The banker mulled over the idea, then made up his mind. "A bank can't make a habit of handing over money to people based on their word," he explained, "but in your case, I'm willing to take a chance. I've heard of the work you're doing at Cordia. After talking with you, I believe you're worth the risk." Alice left Hindman with four hundred dollars in her pocket.

The money was soon gone, but it lasted long enough to buy windows and the supplies needed to erect the building. Alice sketched a drawing of the cabin and went over it with the workhands. "Now, we need rain and lots of it," she told them, imagining a river of logs. They agreed.

Several times each day, Alice looked skyward. All she saw was a beautiful, clear blue sky dotted with white, puffy clouds. "No rain clouds in sight," she moaned. Normally, clear skies pleased her, but not now. She wanted rain. She desperately needed rain.

One evening as Alice was walking home, she felt a few sprinkles. The tiny raindrops felt like soft kisses as they fell upon her outstretched hands. "Mother Nature is being kind," Alice thought.

However, the rain was only a spring shower, much to Alice's dismay. She didn't have time to dwell on the dry weather. Instead, she went about her way teaching classes, writing letters, and planning with the workhands.

A week later, Mother Nature brought a smile to Alice's face. The rain began in the early morning and lasted through the night. A tide flooded the banks of Lotts Creek. The time was right to float logs down the creek from John Riley Kelly's sawmill. Mill workers and cabin builders teamed up to roll the logs into the rushing stream.

Alice watched men float logs downstream. Workers pushed and pulled logs that washed up on the creek bank until they were back in the water. Other times they dislodged logs that caught on bridges and rocks. When the logs floated all the way down to Cordia, the men snagged them out of the creek into a huge pile. Then they dragged the logs, one by one, up the hillside to the cabin site. Aching backs and sore muscles plagued the workers by the time they went home that night.

By then, Alice had all the rain she needed. The sky was blue and the future looked clear for her settlement school. She didn't see the dark clouds hovering over the horizon.

The library – first building at Lott's Creek Community School

Alice's log cabin – used as girls' dormitory, classroom, and home

Chapter 12
THE DREAM LIVES ON

Alice chose the name Lotts Creek Community School and looked on with pride at the school's first building, a library. A dozen books lined one shelf. Alice's friends from the summer camp in Canada and the schools in Ohio had begun to send supplies. Soon books poured in like water rushing down a steep mountain stream.

Word of Alice's settlement school spread. More students came each year – and more students created the need for more teachers. Alice reached out to her younger brother, Bob, who had stayed with the Bacon family and gone to school in Cleveland. "Bob, why don't you move to Cordia and teach here?" Alice asked. Bob considered her offer and accepted it. By the fifth year, the high school had twenty-eight students and three teachers. Year after year, as the number of students and teachers grew, so did the settlement school.

Alice's new home was a cabin at her settlement school. She was always happy to open the door and talk with students, parents, or neighbors. She was especially happy to open the door for her mother, Leanner, who came to visit Alice often and usually stayed several nights.

"I'm proud of you, Alice," Leanner said. "You're a hard worker. You get things done."

"And I'm proud of you," Alice told her mother. "No one has ever worked harder than you."

Alice was busier than ever. All her life, she spent so much time working, she had little time for herself. Although her dream of building a settlement school was coming true, feelings of loneliness settled over Alice on the day her mother died. To handle her grief, Alice once again turned to the comfort of poetry.

> *Tis June,*
> *Yet autumn*
> *With its pale mist*
> *And silvery winds*
> *Has come.*
> *You smiled,*
> *Touched my hand,*
> *And were gone.*

Alice had friends and workers and family around her, but she longed for a family of her own. Still, Alice thought, "I gave up on the idea of marriage when I returned to Kentucky, and I don't regret that decision. I made a choice and I accepted it."

One day Alice welcomed a New York Times reporter, Robert Stewart, who came to Cordia to write a news story. She and Robert spent hours talking. She enjoyed his companionship and pleasant personality. Robert seemed to be the cure for the loneliness that ailed Alice. She spent more and more time with him, and they soon married.

"I love my work and my personal life is everything I hoped for," Alice told him. Her husband believed in her vision of a settlement school for all the children of the community. She appreciated his encouragement and trusted him.

Trust in people was something that came easily for Alice. Trust began with her parents who loved her very much. Her brothers and sisters had always been there for Alice; she could depend on them. Mrs. Lloyd, at Caney Creek Community Center, was ready to help any way she could. Mrs. Bacon, the woman whose family Alice had lived with in Cleveland, had been trustworthy and continued to write to her often; even as the years passed, if Alice needed someone to talk to, Mrs. Bacon and her daughters were willing to listen. The Bacon sisters visited Alice at Cordia to show their support. Mrs. Case, the wilderness camp director, had proven to Alice repeatedly that she could be trusted. The people in the community at Cordia had earned her trust, so much so that they became her extended family.

Before meeting Robert Stewart, Alice had not had any great reason to distrust people. Maybe that's why she never doubted her husband when he said the money he spent came from his work at the newspaper. Her trust in Robert ended the day Alice saw him remove money from the small box that belonged to the very school she struggled so hard to build. When she confronted Robert, he lied to her.

"Stealing and lying are the last things I would have expected from the man I married," Alice said. "I trusted you completely." For her, trust was the true measure of character. Robert had betrayed that trust.

Alice realized she really didn't know her husband at

all. "You are not the person I thought you were," she told him. Alice soon divorced Robert and decided to spend the remainder of her life focused on building the settlement school.

Cordia High School grew quickly. Students worked in the new classrooms and found even more to learn in the book-filled library. The hills surrounding Cordia became the science lab as Alice took her students on nature walks.

With gentle manner and soft voice, Alice taught hungry minds about snakes and other creatures of the wild. Pupils stared in awe as she got a forked stick, stuck it behind the head of a black snake, then picked it up and stroked it. She taught students about the country that lay far beyond the mountains. She taught them to ask questions and seek answers.

If students misbehaved, Alice settled matters with talk. If teachers had problems, she talked with them. If community members had complaints or suggestions, she talked with them. Her speech was always gentle, but no one doubted her toughness.

As the school grew, Alice became the principal. She spent days encouraging students to dream big and to work hard to achieve their dreams. She taught them to be courteous and keep their word. She spent afternoons guiding students who stayed in the two dorms: boys in the building on the left side of her house and girls on the right. She encouraged students to respect the earth, to pick up trash, to clean the environment. She spent evenings writing letters to friends, telling them of her students.

Newspapers carried the story of Alice's settlement

school far and wide. People came to visit, and Alice met with each visitor. They walked around the campus, met students, and looked at the flowers Alice had planted around each building.

Alice never married again, never had children of her own. But through the years, she had a parade of children who walked the halls of her settlement school and looked to her for guidance, care, and affection.

Alice proudly announced, "I am going to work until I'm eighty years old." And she did, enjoying new adventures each day. She watched her settlement school grow, student by student, building by building, teacher by teacher. Today, with a staff of twenty-eight teachers and almost three hundred students from preschool through high school, Alice's dream lives on.

During her lifetime, Alice's adventures carried her out of the hills to get an education and back to the hills to share it. Her greatest adventure carried her over the hills to the narrow valley of Lotts Creek. And it is there that her adventure lives on to this very day with each student that walks through the doors of the high school at Cordia.

Alice's dream has grown into this 21st Century high school at Cordia, Kentucky

Alice looks over the campus of her school

Epilogue
THE SETTLEMENT SCHOOL LEGACY

Early in the 1900's one-room schools dotted the Kentucky hills. The community schools had classes for students in grades one through eight. High schools were scarce at the turn of the 20th Century.

Settlement schools provided an education to mountain children. Students lived at school through the week, even longer if their homes were far away.

In 1902, May Stone and Katherine Pettit established Hindman Settlement School, located in Knott County, Kentucky. The school became a model for other settlement schools, such as Cordia in 1933.

Settlement schools worked with the community as well as with students. The community helped build the school; in turn, the school educated the community's children. At times, the school provided all the needs of each student – food, shelter, clothing, and an education. Some schools taught classes such as sewing to adults, as well.

Settlement schools were based on the same idea as settlement houses. Jane Addams started the most famous settlement house, Hull House, in Chicago in 1889.

Settlement houses established kindergartens, taught classes to citizens in the community, and encouraged people to improve roads, housing, and living conditions.

When Alice Slone visited Hull House, she was impressed with the operation and later utilized many of those ideas at Lotts Creek Community School. She believed that educators must deal with the total child, insisting that a child who is cold or hungry cannot be taught. Her style of progressive education caught the attention of newspaper editors, who told her story.

Educated women who established settlement schools were true pioneers. They began with nothing more than a dream, an idea. They had no books to teach them how to get the job done; they learned by doing. Few jobs were available to educated women in the early part of the 20th Century, so being the true pioneers they were, women such as Alice Slone and Alice Lloyd created jobs for themselves.

Lotts Creek Community School, now called Cordia, was the last settlement school built in Eastern Kentucky. As more schools, better roads, and transportation improvements developed, the need for settlement schools lessened. These schools were valuable to the people of the mountains. Some students learned skills to help them find jobs, and others went on to college; many of them returned to the mountains to serve as teachers, doctors, lawyers, and business leaders.

Alice died in 1994, but her spirit lives on as another of her dreams came true with a new school building for her beloved Cordia. Four years after her death, students at Cordia moved into a modern building, where a large library is lined with books, a computer lab connects students to the world, and a science lab is filled with equipment, always ready for experiments. Classrooms, from preschool through high school, bustle with students. A scholarship program has been set up to give financial assistance to every graduate so students can continue their studies at colleges or technical schools.

The changes at Cordia School are dramatic, but the birth of a new school building also gave a rebirth to the old school building. It is now home to projects that benefit the community: volunteers assist with home repairs; the Santa Program provides Christmas gifts to every student; a thrift shop offers clothing and household items to those in need.

Introducing students to cultural arts was an ongoing goal of Alice Slone. Now, Alice Whitaker (Alice Slone's niece) is director of the settlement school and continues the tradition that Alice began when she first rang the silver bell. Arts events, such as professional music, plays, and dance performances, are woven into the educational programs that keep Alice Slone's dream alive and well to this very day.

Alice Slone talks with her niece, Alice Whitaker, who is now director of the school

Louisville Courier-Journal photo

Alice uses nature to teach science to students

About THE AUTHOR

Nancy Kelly Allen enjoys digging up facts and weaving them together to tell the life stories of people who intrigue her.
She finds research fascinating because something new is always out there waiting to be discovered.
Entering the minds and hearts of the subjects of her biographies has taught her to appreciate going back in time to places in history that can only visited through literature.

Her careers as social worker, teacher, and librarian have provided a creative base to nurture her love of putting pen to paper.

Nancy is the author of several children's books.
Her picture book, On the Banks of the Amazon, won the award for APPALACHIAN BOOK OF THE YEAR in children's literature.

Nancy was born in Kentucky and lives in the same log cabin in which she grew up.
She has a Master's degree in Education from Morehead State University and a Master's in Library and Information Science from the University of Kentucky.

She lives with her husband, Larry, and her two canine writing muses, Pippin Pooh and Harrietta Scattercat.

Nancy enjoys hearing from her readers.
She can be contacted on her website: www.NancyKellyAllen.com.

Printed in the United States
132263LV00001B/14/P